poems
GINA TRON

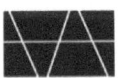

Star 67 ©2020 by **Gina Tron**. Published in the United States by Vegetarian Alcoholic Press. Not one part of this work may be reproduced without expressed written consent from the author. For more information, please contact vegalpress@gmail.com

Cover art by Eleanor Hazard

DIAL UP
Submersion..7
Class Exercise..11
Tsunami..12
Star 67..13
Boat House 15
Your Moth..16
Rule Number 3...17
The Dome...18
Slut Clock...19

BUSY SIGNAL
Eggs..27
Home Economics..28
Dreamscape..29
Shedding...30
Let Me In..31
The Gate.. 33
Busy Signal..34
Mellonella...35
My Concrete...37
Grand Theft Auto...39

RE-ROUTING
Bellicose Butterfly..43
Gotta Look Good..46
Sticky..47
Another Week in America..49
In Bloom...51
Trench coat...52
Black Out..54
Pulsar..55
My Vows...57
Wolf-Rayet..59

GT Phone Home

Star 67 is dedicated to William S. Bonnie: thanks for believing in me. Your presence is missed and we all hope you are watching Space Jam in the afterlife.

Big thanks to Rachel Abramowitz and Chrystin Ondersma for helping me shape this book.

DIAL UP

Submersion

    Accumulation
  dark wet

       dialing

screeching static

      a faceless man running

         helicopter dinosaurs

            attached

    like the start of a movie

[Do you want to die, Sydney?]
   seething through
    distortion
   from phone line
   to
   [I'm inside the house]

He's towering
grabbing
slamming
  blade
across

        jawline
        throat

Lush greens now
in night mode

        He becomes one
        with the boot up

                        [The killer's here, he's in the house]

Her attempted murder
        an extended remix a
        macabre serenade of
        homicidal foreplay
        banter   trivia
        dripping in
        semen-coated lava

Build up of adrenaline
in the volcano
of a sternum
        ready to erupt
        masked figures
        dangle from cord
        to knife:
                impressing
                enticing dries
                up, cracks

        The dance is over

It's just a knife going
into a body now &
daymode floats in
through
white   lace
veiled curtains

The blood spills
        on
           my lap

in electric blue:

[I'm going to rub against you in the hall this week] [to get your scent on me]

        DING

        lower the volume
                eels of smoke
                slither in
                      from a small window
                      my legs sticking

                        [Who are you?]

            a crimson question

A minnow
swimming beside
me in a tank
        a filter forever unchanged?

                                                                    or
STATIC

        Part of the
        school but one
        morphing into
        apex predator
        honing in
        or
        a red herring
        in a pond
miles beyond?
                through a navy blue screen
                      [I'm gonna corner you in the locker room]

Serrated proclamations
sweltering in the heat
        in the distorted chat logs of
        modem
        of mind
        who never entered the house

Brushing against my shoulder
        blowing up
    the transformer
        in my lungs
                gills of a locker slipping
                out of a white bra

    Secret   surrounded by bubbles.

Class Exercise

Dragged down
       from the lockers
       under the

                  UNCLICK

Breathe

                  CLICK

All their paws
       grabbing at the flesh
       of my cheek
       wrapped in bubblegum pink B.U.M Athletic
       illuminated by sun
       reeking of ketchup
       on the same floor

                  [I sat alone on the bleachers
                  in the dark
                  three days before]

Not to be engraved on binders
       I'm the wad of gum under the desk.

Tsunami

       Beneath blue and white cotton

                              plaid and peaches
                                     pencil shavings
              bologna and bleach.

Youth
       and death and
           body odor.

                              A dial tone
                              a conversation
                              covered in onyx squares.

       Navy blue and crimson.

Never been kissed,
sitting on the blue grass
with black wires connecting my brain
to the blasts and crashes

               of roses: pheromones blooming
               in the halls of my mind.

Star 67

Echo of a dial tone
        of a clock in rewind,
                Star 67 & Star 69

        Breath
            so baited
        I'm choking on mine.

                        The first ring
                        The second
                        The third

The click

          That breath

              low and dewy

  3 : 5 8

      pm

                    it's normal, it's fine,

        please let me get to bed
        before the line goes dead.

A screen name

wrapped in fabric and tape
down dark
line and lane.

Boat House

Alone in a boat house
        Through smoke screen
        a protagonist's mirror
        an extra floating.

        On foot there are butterflies
        but in night level
        after the phone collects
        to your underbelly
        the flies emerge from the bog.

                Clogged guitar riffs
                a throat stuffed with kelp
                coyotes yelp from your crotch
                in the most cinematic of ways.

                Young forever in a bottle
                strangled with tape
                heart breaks into bubbles
                as you hide your digits
                from the break of day.

Your Moth

Under the haze
       of open lids
       and under the lines
       you traced
Wings on my wrist
as the sky broiled
       waves baked
       the corners
       of our cove
       on the cliff
             of waking life.

A flip of the switch
       and I'll fly to you
through tunnel and cave
through screen and welcome netting.

Webbed and ready

                            [to be filled with electricity]

the jolt of your IP address
       as I screenshot
       succumb to your messages.

Rule Number 3

'Gremlins' taught me

1. Don't eat after midnight
2. Don't get wet
3. Light can kill

It's all true.

Once I got attracted to a car's dome light
and I almost died.

Inside the Dome

Still
        like a blade of grass
        under ambivalent prints of white

        The wind blew
                fast & cold
        and the lines froze over

        Ice wed me to the blade
                into one
                      indifferent to being mowed down.

Slut Clock

First hand rolls back
to Nintendo's
White Men Can't Jump

                                                                                  fast forward

                             to drawings of
                                    sluttish time
          like Edgar Allen Poe
jokes about violence,
                [it was just a nerd reference
                not a sex reference]
from a time
        I could not be thought of as a slut.

                  Tick
                          tock

I am called
    a slut

                                    during time

and time

                          time

after time

                                    and time.

          Turn a hand back

      to the bar   for a book club meeting but I had to say bar
                                    who in their right mind
                                    would believe someone with wild hair
                                    could read books?
No nerd, only slut in bar now
To the courtroom,   wind up

                    where it struck twelve

                                        my glass slipper
                                            full of cocaine
                                                crushed

        under the wheels
                    of a car,
            driven by a man
with eyes of glass.

                    Pushed
                        into clocking back in.

                [Father time: work until you die,
                you are nothing
                but a tick in time.]

                        Level 3
            I die
                        and now
                        the time has come
        to play

the same levels again

                                        [More knowledge
                                        less interest]

      I die

                    Warp to Level 5
                                        knock on his door
                IF I DID IT

                    [I could march into
                    the NYPD's SVU unit]
                    At 4

                    with a knife and glove
                                      or 3

for the special victims
                    but only on TV

                    [If only the show
                    showed what they really did]

                            look for that detective
                            who said I dressed like a slut
force him to dress
                    like I did
                              which was not slutty
                              (by the way)
                    but IF I DID

                                            who cares.

          Violent sex
          would be the ultimate crime
          if it came from inside my pink mind,

it'd decrease my value
from
          7
                        to

                                        3

down from 9
and nobody under 4
is even allowed
on the courtroom floor.

                Guess what.

              Officer.
                    I get hit.

                        Sometimes
                        when it's a quarter past two.

     It wasn't a sex thing
     it was a nerd thing.

              IT CAN BE BOTH

JUROR JUROR JUROR JUROR JUROR
(Please listen) JUROR JUROR JUROR
JUROR JUROR JUROR

                  Time's up
                        Time's the slut.

                Too quiet,
                        the clock keeps ticking

        in nightmode
                hard wired
until the second hand
hits six.

                Too bold

7
        nines jabbing the room
        sixes stabbing the condensation

too embedded
                                clock ticks too loud

        It's 11

        nobody wants to hear
                        or look

[A man I have been sleeping with said whenever he watches mating scenes in nature shows the males are always doing something abusive to the females, we women are hardwired to like that, he told me, after I let him slap my face.]

        Hardwired
            and batteried up
for the bedroom
the courtroom
the interrogation room
with nothing but handcuffs
and a clock on the wall
set to a different time than mine.

       Can be reset
       Can try it all again

until 3:53

   BLINK

       neon in a dark car
       after I return to that bar

trying to level up
after the reset.

       My batteries
       are in the dump
       next to a blown out
       video game cartridge.

BUSY SIGNAL

Eggs

        Broken   links
                [of an Angelfire page]
neon gifs
    dripping sage
over a parallel dimension.

Broken wings
    of an angel costume
    as the sky turns into an Easter egg
    baby pink & blue hues

        [sucking a pacifier
        sprawled on blanket
        mobile of felt]
after eating
a bad egg
a brown egg
        [fizzled fever up my veins
        draped in Skittles and Pez
        a drop of pink
        and I swirled into yellow]
& soon I'm diaperless
peeing all over an ICU bed.

Reborn
from hard-boiled
to getting wrapped in plastic
    & I can live on in a JPEG in an abandoned hyperlink.

Home Economics

Eggs
milk, sugar, salt
vanilla extract
pulse in a blender.

The first fire
I could touch.

                I wasn't allowed
                to try it at home.

Cyanide baking inside
Mom's casserole dish.

Her ingredients drained
crushed by blades
        [fear and flour
        permeating
        her veins.]

In a few years,
mushrooms on toast
        [I'm supposed to know
        how to cook.]

The home work
I drove home:
        simmering
        boiling thoughts
        with household products.

Dreamscape

A tube from one
               consciousness to another.

If I dream about them
they're dreaming about me too.

I'd try to control my dreams
shifting settings
like a film director
my mind's screen flickering
images into yours.

      We could sit on a couch
      in a living room
      talking into the night
      under six moons
      walk hand in hand
      as the village goes up in flames.

      And we could hang
            even when
                   I had preserved my pride like jam
                         and stored it away for the winter
                         on the shelves alongside
                         my favorite movies of us.

When you only exist
in the reels
I won't set my alarm anymore.

Shedding

Walls of pink
an umbrella in my hand,
a sex offender's drink.

The first dream
I could control
I dragged cartoon TNT
into the beam
of the ballet studio.

A tutu
but no dance
      the song to take over
      to wear the pants.

An apple
glazed in glitter
stuffed with crystals.

Bleeding wall
as a dad
entered the pink room
during feeding
as a mom ended
her seedling
but yours are angelic
I'm sure.
Your god, too.

      This garden sucks,
      I don't want to be
      the girl gouging her own
      eyes out on the train track
      covered in weeding.

Peeling a layer of skin off
with the wind
as siren lights
weave onto my eyelids.

Let Me In

The day
has pitched
into an onyx canvas
        blank and moonless
        loops instead of stars
staggering
on the wet grass
crushing wounded blades
there's been a slaughter
green leaf volatiles.

The lava below
could open
and swallow me up
as a spaceship
of peepers deflate
        screaming
        drowning
            in my ear canal.

I'd choke on dirt
and melt
before anyone
knew I sank
I'm sure.

Can't find the door,
or even a window
feeling up
your empty home's
vinyl siding
        as the spring storm
        rolls up
        my sternum
        and the wind
        it feels like fall
        about to crystalize
        about to dry up.

I left them open

                                                                                [my windows]

and the sirens are going off:
a severe weather warning.

The green's
gonna rot
into ashes again.

Your moonstone landline
                keeps calling me.

Ring after ring, breath after breath.

                I know it's there,
                dormant
                under the dust
and

                I just want to rip

                              the siding apart

                                          and get inside

before the wind
tears off my skin.

The Gate

Knee deep
and boiled
in that sauce
I stand at your gate
       toe nails calling into dirt
              digging into the voicemails.
              [If I could reverse time, I'd undelete them and
              blast them into your house with a megaphone]

Scrapped & gifted,
I know you're still watching
from your window
and its
rotting shutters
hoping
I'll lay
dying again
       shuttering.

Your shutters
full of termites
your apple
       [the upside down, the rules, the
       reigns, the waters and the call]
full of worms.

Busy Signal

        No more fingering
                of numbers
                        flipping 6 into 9.

Resetting my alarm
        to wake in twilight
        solo in field
surrounded by blowing blades
wailing of creature
from forbidden dialings.

A bolt over a mountain
        and the outline of a beast
illuminated through seconds
before rolling under
Draining numerical pulp into my hourglass shoe.

To be blown up
when it all strikes midnight.

Mellonella

Fluttering through voltage
galvanometric heat
cranked
until the sun peers out
the cracks of my eyes
ultraviolet rays
          [U-turn]
jamming the light
down my throat.

Adjust the brightness
until they're comfortable
    to violet
    and then lilac
    and a pale purple so pale
    it's practically white.

Adjusting until the
salt water
drips down the candlestick
and the bark is ripped off the tree
and my drawers
    once oak
    now plastic
are disorganized
again,
socks strewn,
the tape on the back
of the poster
lost its stickiness
lavender melts
into curdled milk
a palace rots
back to a dorm room.

Dimmed
and off they go
to find a brighter light
or wait
on their own
for their own
to burn out.

My Concrete

       Sunny side up
       cheeks down
              sickly sweet
              peach fuzz
              under white ribbons
              and a galaxy of dust.

       Nervous system was jammed with diamonds
       brain cells ringing
       glistening
       the sole behind my lids.

       He helped me repaint my columns
       once beaming from the clouds,
       but now,
       just a lampshade,
              upholstered in polyester
              appliqued with a fawn
              eating clover in a pasture.
       Dust rests upon rim.

       Diamonds dulled.
                            [They were never real
                            & I prefer sea glass anyway.]

       After those children were massacred (on the day of love),
              he spent 12K on machine guns
              instead of my lavender sapphire.

[italic lavender: It is not going to bloom.]
                                          EJECTED
Coral linens blow
and
I blew away from
it all,
the flurries
the subzero.

But,

A dusty phone call and

      I melt
      like a snowflake on a hot windshield.
          A few minutes intertwined
          like a tight Chiffon thread
          equals sheets and sheets of the fabric in my mind.

      Big and unfoldable
      splayed,
      pretty and pink and
      & it covers up some of the concrete.

Grand Theft Auto

                        Childhood suspended,
we walk under sherbet skies
      past homes
      past cages.
                              Crackles and pops
    belly on ground

          crawling towards a Buick

                    [a memory of a red-bellied snake on dirt]
                    slithering under

        the loudest gunshot
            pierces
            ears
            both our hearts
            which slither into one
            beet red pool.

We run towards the noisy street
      shaking, hungry.

We wait an hour
      in a line
      for a video game.

We spend the night
      stealing cars
      and shooting people
      and laughing.

                    Maybe it means something,

My parents once hid under a car
as unmarried kids
as bullets rained
on vacation.

                                      But,

                                                                                    we only date three months.

RE-ROUTING

Bellicose Butterfly

If I get diagnosed with terminal cancer, he says,
I'm gonna mow down
that bitch who rejected me
and whoever else is around, I guess.

If I find out I'm about to die, she says,
maybe I'll gun down my rapist
cram the barrel into his garage
turn on the gas
until his eyes bleed
like the Virgin Mary
because I ain't going down without a fight
without taking down
the one who took me down
and whoever else is there, I guess.

It's the American way.

Down deep into the rug
where the rust-colored honey seeped in
and soaked into
the wood panel beneath it
the third floor
open window
Spring wind,
    [the kind that feels so good
    you want to wilt]
when the pansies start to spurt
and the green erections
shoot from the earth,
the dirt,
and the sounds of the overpass
    (the loneliest breeze
    that ever forced its way
    into my ears)
filled with
so many beings
on wheels,
a wave of white noise

rumbling on the shore.

Wave after wave
car after car
and I'm just a pebble
on a burnt beach.

I lay there
like roadkill
the sun moving into
my bedroom wall
peering through
yellow, stinging
down the hall
before shifting
to hover over cold concrete
cascading shade
on a fox
sleeping under a bridge
in the industrial area
waiting and passing.

If I manage to make it to 76
I'm gonna smash my car into a grocery store.
        Broken glass
        and potato chips
        and flowers
        a pond of milk
        and coupons all over the floor
& then I'll act cute
& pretend I meant to hit the brakes.

It's what keeps me going,
fuels me.

The crimson fantasies
come as the grinding
of the wheels
below me accelerate

moving my stomach forward.
        Propane and paraffins
        and papillons.
My brain's oiled up
lubed up to morph
about to take flight.

I hope the fertilizer
drenched in iron-flavored water
helps my lilacs erupt
blooming on the windowsill
across from an overpass
with cars as bright as butterflies.

Gotta Look Good

When I got into that car crash
I turned down my music.

                        [They can't hear me listening to that
                        and why am I wearing this?]
There's an ambulance
        red lights flashing
            [but why am I wearing this?]

A Sunday morning outfit
not my Tuesday afternoon best
                        [not even eyeliner]
but the guy
whose car I crashed into
later told me

                I looked good.

My friend told me
when her school was getting shot up
and she was fleeing the building
after the guy was killed
she made sure
to adjust her hair
as she ran by the security cams

        just in case
           footage of her
               was included on the nightly news.

When I die
I now want
my entire internet search history
unveiled at my funeral.

I'm nobody's beloved daughter
or mother
or spouse.

Sticky

Pink plumes and bad breath
transparent carbon dioxide snakes
mouth to trunk,
brighter, greener, angrier, bolder
the yellow light
in between red and green
                looking for permanent parking.

Over switching sides
every third day
so the street can be swept of grime.

[Reminder]
      No power
      even when you think.

      You're green and shiny
      until you cross the line
      and then you're red
      and towed away.

You can light yourself up
so they don't slither away
but never ever forget
you're the one being hunted.
                [Even if you hold a gun,
                    you don't get to decide
                        who's chasing you.]

Keep driving
even when the light is red,

the snake
wrapped around their trunk.

Exfoliate all you want

you're not Adam
and I'm definitely not Eve.

I'm too weak
until my hand slithers past 7
then I'm too intimidating
and the electrical box
is ripped up
the wires
snake around my fingers
stick into my brain.

Another Week in America

Just another
7-day span
another unremarkable
collection of days
unfolding.

I screenshot a news story
and sent it to a friend
before reading it.
Isn't this crazy?
Look at this headline
and then
I actually looked
and oh yeah
I know that guy,
he used to brag
about knowing me
and now I have
to make some calls,
and my phone is dying
dammit,
I wanted to buy a
a new shirt
but
I guess I have to go home
and do the right thing now.

I spend three hours
sifting through emails
and Facebook messages
to make sure a dead teen
[a rotting Columbine flower
who doesn't understand
that her obsession
would have killed her
and walked over her body
without guilt]
isn't one of the troubled kids
who messaged me in 2013

because the Narcissist flower
blooming in my belly
is scared she read
some things I wrote
and
I don't want to
have to feel guilty
about any
thing,
I wanted to
consume things
and buy things
and look at living flowers instead.

A friend tells me
she witnessed
someone getting shot
in the face
on Easter Sunday
as the cities darkened
to see Game of Thrones.
Treat yourself, I tell her.
If you see someone get murdered
I suppose you deserve
to murder your bank account,
buy yourself something nice
like a child labor shirt.
If you can't pamper yourself
after that
then when can you
I guess?

I used to think killing
was rare
but it's not.
It's dotting the landscape
like pine trees
and Targets.

In Bloom

As the snow dies
unveiling the dirt
and the feces
ready to rot
magnolias blossom
and refrigerated rage
thaw outs
ready to bloom.

Just released
from Arctic cages
ready to bite the flowers
that clash with the mood rings.

Salty streams
crystallized
by Instagram filters
pink and lavender milk
flowing down bark.

It's a diseased rainbow
not one ray
but seven
I can't look away
from the beauty
of destruction
of a cherry blossom tree
getting hacked up:
porn
for the sickest part
of my heart.

Trench Coat

I wish
I wish
I could make these
memories stick
from the trenches.

New experiences
roll off like raindrops sliding
down Gore-Tex
to soak up worms
on the pavement
on an April morning driveway
dewy and doe-eyed.

Once
was porous
my skin
raw
and uncovered
drops dug in like ticks.

I had to protect
my skin rivers
from that
swirling storm
in my head
and above it
winds and strikes—
I can't take this coat off.

I stepped in a puddle
        on purpose
& I'm swimming in experiences
but they dissolve

like disappointing clouds.

Walking through the world
with red paint dripping
from my jacket:
sometimes it's success.

Sometimes it's trauma.

Black Out

While oiled in gasoline
        holes in my memory
        a brain like Waco
                puncture wound by wound.

Christmas lights twinkling
through the sweat
of the night
smoke and heat
until all I saw was white.

Not quite raining
the condensation could crush my jaw
        leaning on a brick wall
                under neon cross
slurring into a dream
kissing
another human
in another dimension
space and time
        stars falling slowly
        pink crushed up dust.

A deep swamp
beyond the forest
and a black hole
with so much
fire inside
a body filled with coal
caked in cold oatmeal.

A turquoise gown
on the boardwalk
at night
standing in the rain
gripping
a busted umbrella
getting ready for
the tsunami to hit.

Pulsar

        I steal his luminosity
        in the backseat of my
        neutral Toyota Camry
                crickets mask
                our aurora:
                steamy
                stars in heat.

        He pulls me,
        we run across wet grass
                under the Big Dipper
        to fuse in the farmhouse
        drenched in salt water.

        We will never be aligned,
        but we keep using our telescopes
        to pull each other
        into our electromagnetic fields.

        Me and him
                but also you and me.

        Rapidly rotating,
        years mean nothing to us.

We love in hyperspace
        hesitate with hyperactivity.
        Fleeting caresses,
        arms over mine
we pulsate under the moon
he wants to own me
        for hours, centuries, still
        just like the others burning up in the milky way.

        Aren't you proud of me?

                I learned from the best.

          I stole his brick
so
stop stalking me and KoolAid my wall.

My Vows

Too cute
to walk the street
without the realistic fear
of getting raped
a 6/10 piece of loot
of meat
from the white ties in my jean shorts
ready to greet
standing at a payphone
simmering heat
in wait
to that argyle dress
over an October grate
texting an address
car keys
to house keys
jammed between my fingers
like claws
combating bait.

But
too ugly,
only a Friday taste
and more importantly
too weird
just waste
to ever expect
to have
a normal life
a speech, King bed, toothpaste
alluring enough
to make them obsess
but not enough
for the rest,
it will always
be the edge of a sunset
and a cliff's edge
complete unrest.

Too narcissistic
to put myself
on the discount shelf,
why would I?
I know my worth,
even if these idiots don't.

It's probably too late
Daddy Time has
destroyed me
from behind the blinds
cut me into patches
but I'll be fine
& also damned
if that will stop me.

Wolf-Rayet

A raven battleaxe
engraved on each tooth
still chattering over a battleground:
dust and bodies and blood.

Iron and gun power
still in my nostrils,
hairless and lined with polyethylene.

The same grassy field
where cannons bloomed nightshades
in their shadows.

I'm howling at my reflection under
an exploding sky
red and furious
fading
nitrogen
on jailbreak
from spinal encasements.

Soon I'll be dead on the highway
cars passing

as I rot.

Please believe
I'm atop canyons
with my pack
and the sky so clear.

Gina Tron has authored several books, including *You're Fine.* (2014) and *Eggolio and Other Fables* (2015). She has two books forthcoming: *Employment*, which will also be published by Vegetarian Alcoholic Press, and *Suspect*, a non-fiction book with Tarpaulin Sky Press, which won their 2020 book award. Her poems have been published in *Green Mountains Review, Hunger Mountain, Junto Magazine* and *Tupelo Press*. Gina has an MFA in Writing and Publishing from the Vermont College of Fine Arts. In addition to writing true crime content for *Oxygen*, her reporting has been in the *Washington Post, VICE, Daily Beast* and *Politico*.

www.ingramcontent.com/pod-product-compliance
Lightning Source LLC
Chambersburg PA
CBHW022014120526
44592CB00034B/950